APHRODITE

A PLAY

JAMES M. GUIHER

iUniverse, Inc.
New York   Bloomington

Aphrodite
A Play

This is a work of fiction. All of the characters, names, incidents, organizations, and dialogue in this play are either the products of the author's imagination or are used fictitiously.

No professional or nonprofessional performances of any kind or in any media of this play may be given without the permission of the author, who can be contacted at: jamesmguiher.com

iUniverse books may be ordered through booksellers or by contacting:

iUniverse
1663 Liberty Drive
Bloomington, IN 47403
www.iuniverse.com
1-800-Authors (1-800-288-4677)

Because of the dynamic nature of the Internet, any Web addresses or links contained in this book may have changed since publication and may no longer be valid. The views expressed in this work are solely those of the author and do not necessarily reflect the views of the publisher, and the publisher hereby disclaims any responsibility for them.

ISBN: 978-1-4502-4805-1 (sc)
ISBN: 978-1-4502-4806-8 (ebook)

Printed in the United States of America

iUniverse rev. date: 08/12/2010

Characters

Ben Hastings

Helen Hastings

Silvia

Xenia

Setting:

A room bare except for a full-sized white plaster copy of the Aphrodite of Melos stage right and a couch facing it, a table, and a floor lamp. The back of the room is ringed with strips of black cloth. Entrances and exits are made between the sections of cloth. A spotlight shines on the statue throughout the play, rising and lowering in intensity as indicated.

Scene i

Ben is standing by the couch. Casually dressed in a tweed jacket, rumpled pants and a button-down shirt with no tie, he looks like the middle-aged college professor he is as he stares intently at the statue, brightened by an overhead spotlight. Slowly circling, he carefully examines the statue from every angle. He crosses to the table beside the couch, opens a drawer, removes a tape measure, returns to the statue, and measures the distance between her breasts. HELEN enters. A handsome woman in her mid-forties, she watches him measure the distance from the statue's breasts to her navel and from her navel to her crotch. BEN pulls a small notebook from his coat pocket and writes down the measurements.

HELEN

Ben.

(He frowns at the figures in his notebook.)

I'm sorry to bother you.

(He pulls out the tape and places the end of it in Aphrodite's navel.)

BEN

Here, hold this.

(She grasps the tape as he stretches it up to Aphrodite's left breast, checks the distance and glances at his notebook.)

Now the other one.

(He measures the distance up to her right breast, looks at his notebook, then has HELEN move the tape up to her right breast so he can measure the distance across to her left breast. Referring to his notebook, he scowls and shakes his head.)

HELEN

Is there something wrong?

BEN

The distance between her breasts and from her breasts to her navel and from her navel to her crotch are all supposed to be equal.

HELEN

Is that it? I've often wondered why you find her so fascinating.

BEN

The downward angle between her breasts throws it off.

HELEN

You're the only person in the world who cares about the space <u>between</u> them.

BEN

What appears to be a realistic torso is actually constructed with great geometrical precision.

HELEN

If you ask me, I say her breasts are rather small, for a woman her size. Of course, now she could easily have that deficiency corrected.

BEN

With their acute eye for geometrical relationships, the Greeks created the classic proportions that have become the standard of beauty ever since.

HELEN

You mean we're all supposed to look like that?

BEN

Nature of course rarely follows the laws of classic proportions.

HELEN

How far off am I?

(She stretches the tape across her chest.)

BEN

You're fine.

HELEN

I'd really like to know.

BEN

It only applies to works of art.

HELEN

It's just another way to make women feel there's always something wrong with us.

BEN

No woman can hope to be perfect.

HELEN

But she is?

BEN

The Greeks thought so.

HELEN

I guess the rest of us just have to live with what we've got.

(She cups her breasts.)

Not bad for forty-three.

BEN

Look, I have a lot of work to do.

HELEN

Do you know what today is? Roger's birthday. He's made a special trip from school. Why don't you come home and help us celebrate?

(BEN takes the tape measure, crosses to the table, and drops it into the drawer.)

I haven't told him. I don't know how to explain it.

BEN

You know our agreement.

HELEN

He'll be very disappointed.

BEN

He'll have lots more birthdays.

HELEN

I think you should tell him. If you tell him, maybe he'll understand.

BEN
(Slamming the table drawer.)

Roger?

HELEN

He's matured a great deal now that he's away from home and on his own.

BEN

Still wants to be an engineer doesn't he?

HELEN

You can explain how she's put together just like a well- constructed building.

BEN

You know I can't.

HELEN

Please darling, just for one night. Remember when Roger was ten and after his birthday party he slept over at Ted's.

(She caresses his chest.)

You'd been away for a week at a conference and.. .well we never got to the bedroom but made love there on the couch.

BEN

You agreed you know.

HELEN

Yes, but I didn't realize how difficult it would be to come home from work to an empty house with no one there.

BEN

It's not easy for me either you know.

(SILVIA enters. A lovely young girl whose crisp white uniform barely contains her voluptuous figure, she carries a tray containing a glass and a pitcher of martinis, places the tray on the table, fills the glass, and leaves.)

HELEN

Who's that?

BEN

Silvia.

HELEN

Silvia?

BEN

Everyday at five o'clock she brings me a pitcher of martinis.

(He takes a sip.)

Ice cold and very dry.

HELEN

Is she a nurse? Does she check your blood pressure and give you your pills?

BEN

I don't need them anymore, now that I don't have classes and that asshole of a Dean to contend with.

HELEN

He was good enough to advance your sabbatical so you could come here this spring.

BEN

All right, so he's only a half asshole.

HELEN

Speaking of the Dean, he called yesterday and asked how you were getting along.

BEN
(Turning to the statue.)

You know, it's incredible, everyday I make amazing new discoveries.

HELEN

I said I was coming over today.

BEN

Just this morning I was looking at her and suddenly saw her in an entirely new way.

(Light up on the statue.)

HELEN

He's concerned about you.

BEN

Scientists tell us the universe began with the Big Bang and it's been expanding outwards ever since. As we look up into space, we look back in time, and when we peer at the edge of the universe we see the glow from the Big Bang itself.

HELEN

He wants to know if you'll be gone for the whole six months.

BEN

Civilization began with a kind of big bang, with the glorious wonders of Greece and Rome which then spread out in all directions from the Mediterranean Sea. When we look at Aphrodite, we look back in time and see the glow from the very beginnings of civilization.

HELEN

Ben ...

BEN

And just now I realize we see something else. We see a calmness, a serenity that we yearn for in our world that seems to be flying apart into a thousand different pieces. Through her, we can recapture some of that early spirit that bound us together.

HELEN

You can tell all this to Roger ...

BEN

We forget how old she is ...

HELEN

He loves science fiction.

BEN

And yet how young. Just one of the countless contradictions that makes her a fascinating study of infinite complexity.

(HELEN quietly leaves.)

She knows so much and yet tells us nothing. Another of her maddening contradictions--profound yet silent.

(He circles the statue as if waiting for her to speak, but she says nothing.)

SCENE 2

BEN is sitting on the couch. SILVIA brings in a tray of martinis, puts it on the table and leaves. BEN fills his glass and sits back to contemplate the statue, bathed in medium light. XENIA enters, slim and elegant in a simple black dress with a single strand of pearls dipping across her thin chest. Her black hair, dark complexion, and fine, chiseled features make it difficult to tell her age. In one hand is a cigarette, in the other an empty glass.

XENIA

You must be someone very special. They tell me there's no alcohol allowed in this place and here you are with a whole pitcher of martinis. I've offered them everything, even myself, but I can't find out who you have to sleep with to get a drink around here.

BEN

I'm sorry but I'm very busy.

XENIA

It's five o'clock, time to relax and give the right side of your brain a rest, or is it the left side? I can never remember.

BEN

Please, I must ask you not to interrupt.

XENIA

Don't mind me. I'll just take a little of this. I'm sure you can get more where it came from.

(She fills her glass and looks around for an ashtray. Finding none, she flicks her ashes onto the top of Aphrodite's gown.)

BEN
(Rising.)

What are you doing?

XENIA

Thought that might get her to drop that silly gown. Did you ever wonder about her legs? My guess is they're fat and ugly. Why else would she keep them covered up?

(BEN dusts off the ashes with his handkerchief.)

Sorry, next time I'll bring an ashtray.

BEN

I don't smoke and I'd appreciate if my visitors don't either.

XENIA

It's the only vice they permit here, at least the only one they allow me. Everyone's entitled to at least two, don't you think?

BEN

I don't mean to be rude …

XENIA

Let me guess. You're an artist? No, you're too anal to be an artist. Someone who lives in his head, someone who has orgasms in his brain instead of the way god intended.

BEN

I really must insist …

XENIA

What's the point of living with a statue of a woman?

BEN

She's the object of my research.

XENIA

Ah, a professor?

BEN

Yes.

XENIA

Of anatomy?

BEN

Art history.

XENIA

Art history?

BEN

My specialty is Greek sculpture.

XENIA

And especially the Venus de Milo.

BEN

No.

XENIA

Come on, she's the most famous marble broad in the world.

BEN

She's more properly known as the Aphrodite of Melos. She's Greek, not Roman.

XENIA

I've never understood, what's the big deal with her?

BEN

What looks at first glance like a fairly simple statue is actually a very complex figure.

(Light up on the statue.)

XENIA

When I look at her, I'm so worried her dress is about to fall off that I hardly notice anything else.

BEN

She's so full of contradictions it makes her very difficult to understand.

XENIA

She's a woman. You're not supposed to understand her.

BEN

A woman yes, but one that represents woman freed from the exigencies of time and the contingencies of place, a figure that embodies the essence of woman.

XENIA

The essence of woman?

BEN

The idea that precedes and is immanent in all women.

XENIA

If I had an essence, god forbid, it sure wouldn't be anything like this bimbo.

BEN

She's actually very intelligent.

XENIA

How can you tell?

BEN

In her head is the knowledge and wisdom possessed by all women.

XENIA

Her head? Look how small it is compared to the rest of her.

BEN

It takes a certain amount of intelligence to appreciate hers.

XENIA

Did you ever notice how most people seem reasonably intelligent until they open their mouths?

BEN

Ah, if she could only speak.

XENIA

Obviously the perfect woman – deaf and dumb. And also exposed and helpless, just the way you'd like all women to be if you'd only admit it.

BEN

Aphrodite helpless? She's one of the twelve Olympian gods, daughter of Zeus, sister of Athena and Apollo, mother of Aeneas, the founder of Rome.

XENIA

She'd get a lot more respect if she had some clothes on instead of standing there like some Greek Playboy centerfold.

BEN

She's the goddess of love. She's supposed to be sexy.

XENIA

Sexy? You think this overgrown frigid Amazon is sexy?

BEN

The Greeks certainly thought so.

XENIA

I read somewhere that any mortal who slept with her was condemned to die.

BEN

He could also be castrated or bound to a turning wheel for all eternity.

XENIA

Shouldn't you put up a sign, fooling around with this woman can be dangerous to your health?

BEN

It's only a statue.

XENIA

And a rather boring one at that. An empty, vacuous expression, no arms, fat ass and wide hips, not to mention that silly pose only a fag photographer would dream up.

BEN

The miracle is how they all come together ...

XENIA

It must be the tits. Firm and luscious, you men can feast your eyes on them and pretend you're examining a work of art. What is it with men and boobs? The most enjoyable parts of a woman after all are above and below the chest. Our minds are as sharp and complex as any German's and our pudendums surpass the sensuous delights of Italy, yet men are obsessed with the Swiss Alps in between.

BEN

Her breasts are actually too small, for a woman her size. At least my wife thinks so.

XENIA

You're married?

BEN

I really must get back to work.

(Light down on the statue.)

XENIA

Separated?

BEN

No.

XENIA

You're gay and you decided to come out. It's all the fashion these days.

BEN

A homosexual would hardly be interested in Aphrodite.

XENIA

Gay men love glamorous women. Judy Garland, Maria Callas, why not Aphrodite?

BEN

You'll have to ask them about that.

XENIA

Camille could tell us.

BEN

Who?

XENIA

Camille Paglia. She thinks gay men are the greatest thing since Eve came out brain-damaged from Adam's rib.

BEN

It's women who should learn to admire Aphrodite. She was always in command, never let herself be a victim.

XENIA

It was easy for her, everyone knew you screw her and you die.

BEN

She's at least as good a role model as the other women the feminists keep raving about.

XENIA

I gather your wife does not share your enthusiasm for her.

BEN

I've tried to explain to her that Aphrodite contains many contradictions and mysteries that haven't yet been resolved, but she doesn't really appreciate what I'm trying to do.

XENIA

Maybe there just isn't that much there worth trying to figure out.

BEN

The problem is that women, marvelous creatures that they are, lack the ability to think conceptually. As important as men are in their lives, you would think they would have created a vision of the ideal man, but they haven't.

XENIA

Mainly because there's no such thing.

BEN

Michelangelo had to do it for you with his heroic statue of David.

XENIA

That muscle-bound adolescent. He's not anything I'd ever want for myself.

BEN

A typical female reaction, seeing a sublime creation only in terms of your own personal feelings.

XENIA

If we kept looking for the ideal man, we'd never marry any of you poor creatures and thus put a quick stop to the entire human race.

BEN

Women have never even created an inspired vision of themselves. All the great images of women have been created by men--the Greek Aphrodites, the medieval and Renaissance madonnas, Leonardo's Mona Lisa …

XENIA

Whistler's Mother.

BEN

Titian's Venuses…

XENIA

Disney's Pocahontas.

BEN

The odalisques of Ingres and Matisse.

XENIA

The grotesques of de Kooning and Picasso.

BEN

It's much harder today for artists to envision an ideal woman.

XENIA

I don't know, we've got Marilyn Monroe and Madonna.

BEN

Two tramps who've debased the whole concept of woman.

XENIA

Your beloved Aphrodite was not exactly a virgin you know.

BEN

But she's got one thing none of our celebrity sluts possess. Class, genuine class.

XENIA

Here maybe, but in bed with her latest lover it would be quite a different story.

BEN

For once, try to elevate your mind to a level worthy of the subject.

XENIA

You can't expect her to stay on that pedestal forever.

BEN

You shouldn't look at her as a real woman. She's a symbol.

XENIA

A symbol of love.

BEN

Yes.

XENIA

Which makes her immortal.

BEN

And simple and yet very complicated.

XENIA

Love is complicated only when one day it's gone and you wonder why.

BEN

I wouldn't know …

XENIA

Take it from me.

BEN

You're divorced?

XENIA

Never found the ideal man to marry.

BEN

He doesn't have to be perfect.

XENIA

Ah, there's my problem.

BEN

An attractive woman like you.

XENIA

Flattery will cost you another drink…tomorrow.

(She crosses upstage.)

BEN

What's your name?

XENIA

XENIA.

BEN

XENIA?

XENIA

With an "X."

BEN

That's Greek you know. It means a gift.

XENIA

A gift to a stranger.

(She exits. Staring after her, BEN finishes the last of his drink.)

Scene 3

BEN is sitting on the couch drawing the statue (in medium light) on a large sketch pad. SILVIA enters. BEN continues drawing. SILVIA crosses behind him.

SILVIA

I didn't know you're an artist. What's that supposed to be?

BEN

I'm trying to capture the essential rhythms of the figure.

SILVIA

You can't tell if it's a man or a woman.

BEN

It's a woman.

SILVIA
(Proudly.)

The Venus de Milo.

BEN

No.

SILVIA

It sure looks like all her pictures.

BEN

It's the Aphrodite of Melos. She's Greek, not Roman.

SILVIA

Aphro-dite. Sounds like some kind of African hair-do.

BEN

It means the goddess of love.

SILVIA

I like Venus better. It sounds like you know more romantic.

BEN

It says a lot about our age that we now consider Aphrodite to be merely a symbol of romantic love.

SILVIA

I don't know, isn't all love romantic?

BEN
(Continuing to draw.)

There are many kinds, narcissistic, erotic, agape.

SILVIA

What's that?

BEN

Agape? It means altruistic love, a generalized love for everyone but no one in particular. It comes down from the eucharist, the celebration of God's love for man.

SILVIA

Doesn't God love women too?

BEN
(Irritated.)

Yes of course.

SILVIA

I'm sorry to bother you but I need to know if you want to exercise on Monday, Wednesday, and Friday or Tuesday, Thursday, and Saturday.

BEN

Exercise?

SILVIA

You have a choice of aerobics, running, swimming, or working out.

BEN

I don't do any of those.

SILVIA

But you have to get some kind of exercise.

BEN

Not if I choose not to.

SILVIA

It's required of everyone.

BEN

I have to spend all my time on my research.

SILVIA

Research?

BEN

I'm going to write a book about Aphrodite

SILVIA

A whole book just about her?

BEN

She's deceptive in that she's a great deal more complex than she seems.

(Light up on the statue.)

If you look closely, you'll see that she's a mixture of several contrasting styles. Her classical head, her realistic torso, and her gown shaped like those on the figures on the frieze around the Parthenon. She's a veritable symphony of movements and countermovements that give her a baroque feel in what is still a very classical figure.

SILVIA

You'll have to keep it simple. I never went to college.

BEN

She's a combination of two very different styles, a series of fluid and sensuous curves contained within a rather formal and rigid structure.

SILVIA

Is that why she's so big?

BEN

She's somewhat oversize because she stood beside an outdoor athletic field and had to be seen from a considerable distance.

SILVIA

She sure doesn't look like an athlete.

BEN

She's not. She was there as an inspiration to the men on the field.

SILVIA

Kind of like a cheerleader you mean?

BEN

Yes I suppose, in a way.

SILVIA

But you've got to get really enthusiastic if you're going to be a cheerleader. She doesn't look like she cares who wins.

BEN

She appears to be calm and cool yes, but don't be fooled. Inside she's a seething cauldron of turmoil. Born from the waves of the sea, out of the foam generated by the mutilated testicles of Uranus, she carries those powerful currents still within her as well as the rhythmical surges that course through the bodies of all women, only in her the mighty tides of the sea from which she came are relentless and never-ending.

SILVIA

It's a wonder she doesn't get seasick with all that going on.

BEN

It takes an enormous amount of strength to appear so serene while being so storm-tossed within?

SILVIA

How does she do it?

BEN

You have to understand that she's not like an ordinary woman. She's what we call an idealized figure, a figure so perfectly constructed she can exist only in a work of art.

SILVIA

Why do you want to write about a woman who's so unreal?

BEN

It's the puzzle of her many contradictions. Calm on the outside, full of turmoil within. Young and yet so old. One of the most fascinating of her contradictions is the dichotomy between two entirely different kinds of woman. On the one hand, she's pure and full of nurturing love, rather like what we associate with the Virgin Mary.

SILVIA

The Virgin Mary sure never went around looking like that.

BEN

At the same time, she's a voluptuous figure full of lust and fleshly desire.

SILVIA

That's the Venus part?

BEN

It goes all the way back to Plato, who described the dichotomy as that between the celestial and the vulgar, the sacred and the profane.

SILVIA

Is that the kind of stuff you learn in college?

BEN

You can if you take the right courses.

SILVIA

Sometimes I think I'd like to go to college, but then I figure it's not really for me.

BEN

Everyone should know something about the Greeks. Their ideas provide the foundation for all of western civilization.

SILVIA

But I don't understand half of what I know already.

BEN

Good teachers can help a great deal.

SILVIA

But you learn so much, doesn't it get confusing? I mean like you start thinking she's somehow like the Virgin Mary and you end up in a place like this.

BEN

Which is ideal for doing my research if there weren't so many interruptions.

(Light down on the statue.)

SILVIA

I'm sorry, I won't bother you anymore.

BEN

No, no, I'm glad to have a chance to talk to you. I miss my students. Explaining things to them helps to clarify my own thinking.

SILVIA

I bet you're a very good teacher.

BEN

What makes a good teacher is having good students.

SILVIA

And here's stupid me taking you away from your work.

BEN

You're a whole lot more intelligent than you think. And you're curious. That's the critical element that's missing in so many students today.

SILVIA

Maybe I should think about going to college.

BEN

Definitely you should.

SILVIA

Well anyway thanks for taking up so much of your time.

(She starts to leave.)

BEN

You know, you could help me in my research.

SILVIA

Me?

BEN

In many ways, you're like her, young and beautiful. I'm very interested in knowing what she would say if she could talk. I'd like you to imagine that you're her and tell me what you would say.

SILVIA

I have no idea.

BEN

How does it feel to be the focus of so much admiring attention? Do you enjoy the power that stems from your beauty?

SILVIA

Please, just tell me the days you want to exercise.

BEN

The power to have anything you want?

SILVIA

Is Monday, Wednesday, and Friday okay?

BEN

The power to please, the power to destroy?

(She crosses upstage.)

Tell me, I need to know.

(She exits. BEN turns to contemplate the silence of the statue.)

Scene 4

BEN is lying on the couch. Bright light on the statue. HELEN enters.

HELEN

Ben, Ben, are you awake?

BEN

Hunh.

HELEN

Well at least I'm not interrupting some profound new insight.

BEN

I'm meditating. Get some of my best ideas this way.

HELEN

Sure you're not just getting bored with her?

BEN
(Sitting up.)

Bored? Never. The more I learn, the more I realize I don't know.

HELEN

It's going to take a long time then?

BEN

I don't know. It's hard to concentrate with so many interruptions.

HELEN

Twice. I've been here, twice.

BEN

It's not just you. There are no locks on the doors. People wander in whenever they please.

HELEN

They believe getting to know the others might help.

BEN

Help? I don't need any help.

HELEN

I'm afraid I have some bad news. I've lost my job.

BEN
(Rising.)

Lost your job?

(Light down on the statue.)

35

HELEN

I wanted to do an article about a family that had two hundred cats.

BEN

Two hundred cats?

HELEN

A family in town takes them in and the ASPCA helps pay to keep them.

BEN

Sounds like a great story.

HELEN

I thought so too, but the boss said he didn't want people to know about it because then every town in New Jersey would be sending us their stray cats.

BEN

Other towns should do the same thing.

HELEN

He said you start with cats and then its dogs, rabbits, guinea pigs, ferrets, parrots, and god knows what else until the town is turned into a veritable zoo.

BEN

It would be a great improvement over what's there now.

HELEN

He's always giving me a hard time, so I decided to stand my ground on this one. I said if he wouldn't let me do the article, I'd quit. He said that wouldn't be necessary because I'm fired.

BEN

You'll have to get another job.

HELEN

That won't be easy. He's not likely to give me a very good recommendation.

BEN

You've got to find something.

HELEN

What I plan to do is rent the house.

BEN

Rent the house?

HELEN

That will give us enough income to make up for my lost salary.

BEN

But where will you live?

HELEN

In the house.

BEN

In the house? With a bunch of strangers?

HELEN

It won't be a stranger. It's the Dean.

BEN

The Dean?

HELEN

He and his wife are separating.

BEN

How she's put up with him this long I've never understood.

HELEN

They plan to live apart for a while and try to work things out.

BEN

You're going to live in the house with the Dean?

HELEN

We need the money. This place is expensive you know.

BEN

Surely you can find a job somewhere.

HELEN

I'm tired of writing about struggling mothers and dead-beat dads and delinquent kids and all those goddamned cats. I want to do something really creative.

BEN

Creative? Like what?

HELEN

Like stories, a play, maybe a novel.

BEN

But all you know about are struggling mothers and dead-beat dads and delinquent kids.

HELEN

I know a lot more than that. You were just never interested in hearing about it.

BEN

You know you can't live in the same house with the Dean. Not only is he an obnoxious phony, he has the reputation of going after every woman he can get his hands on.

HELEN

I'm too old for that sort of thing.

BEN

There was Oscar's wife, she must be close to sixty.

HELEN

Are you saying you don't trust me?

BEN

I don't trust him. And you know what everyone in town will think.

HELEN

He married Margery for her money, and if he tries anything she'll know about it and refuse to take him back, which would put an end to the high-flying life style he's become accustomed to. He's not about to jeopardize that by doing anything foolish.

BEN

The Dean in our house? It's out of the question.

HELEN

Don't worry, I can take care of myself.

BEN

You can't do this Helen. I absolutely forbid it.

HELEN

It's already done. He moved in yesterday.

BEN

Yesterday? Tell him you've changed your mind.

HELEN

I can't do that.

BEN

It's my house you know.

HELEN

But I have your power of attorney.

BEN

I'll revoke it.

HELEN

You can't, not for six months.

(She leaves. BEN slumps onto the couch.)

Scene 5

BEN is kneeling down to examine the statue's left foot. Bright light on the statue. SILVIA enters.

SILVIA

Professor, your exercise time will be on Monday, Wednesday, and Friday from ten to eleven o'clock in the morning.

BEN
(Struggling to his feet.)

I'm not going to exercise. I thought I made that clear.

SILVIA

The rules say everyone must exercise.

BEN

I don't give a damn about the rules. I'm the one who decides what I do and don't do here.

SILVIA

You have to exercise unless your doctor says you shouldn't

(Light down on the statue.)

BEN

Tell them I have high blood pressure.

SILVIA

Do you have a letter from your doctor?

BEN

No.

SILVIA

We have to have it in writing.

BEN

I might have time for a quick game of squash.

SILVIA

Squash?

BEN

It's a game you play with a racquet and ball inside a room about the size of this one.

SILVIA
(Looking around.)

I don't think they'll allow that.

BEN

I don't mean here. It takes a special kind of court.

SILVIA
(Referring to a small card.)

Squash. It's not on the list.

BEN

Fine. You don't have squash, I don't exercise.

SILVIA

We might be able to arrange some tennis. There's a club down the street.

BEN

Tennis? Tennis is slow, dumb, and boring.

SILVIA

Have you ever watched Andre Agassi play? He's real exciting to watch.

BEN

Really?

SILVIA

He shaved his chest and his head.

BEN

That's what makes him exciting?

SILVIA

He was married to Brooke Shields.

BEN

Brooke Shields?

SILVIA

You know, the actress. She's real beautiful, kinda like you know his Aphrodite, but they got divorced.

BEN

So his game has gone to pieces.

SILVIA

It did for a while, but now he's number one in the world.

BEN

Which proves you don't need the inspiration of a woman.

SILVIA

No, he's got a new one, Steffi Graff.

BEN

Another Aphrodite?

SILVIA

Well, no, not exactly But she does seem to inspire him.

(BEN gazes at her with the searching intensity he ordinarily reserves for the statue, causing SILVIA to quickly change the subject.)

The rules are you've got to get some kind of exercise.

BEN

Well it won't be tennis. Tennis is to squash as checkers is to chess.

SILVIA

Checkers, I love checkers except my grandmother usually beats me. She says I could be good at it if I really tried. And she's like you, she keeps telling me I should go to college.

BEN

You don't want to spend the rest of your life here do you?

SILVIA

I don't know, I kind of like it here.

BEN

It reminds me of the University, full of oddballs and neurotics who could never survive in the outside world.

SILVIA

Some are a little weird, but then some like you are very nice. Not many people treat me the way you do, I mean you talk to me like I wasn't just a child anymore.

BEN

You're hardly what I would call a child.

SILVIA

I've been thinking about that question you asked me, you know about what she would say if she could talk.

BEN

Yes, yes.

SILVIA

I don't know but it would seem to me the first thing she'd do is ask for her arms back.

BEN

Her arms?

SILVIA

You can't do anything if you don't have arms. You can't put on your clothes or drive or talk on the telephone.

BEN

Yes, it would be difficult.

SILVIA

You can't even feed yourself.

BEN

But you know, my theory is she looks so much better without them.

(Light up on the statue.)

She doesn't have arms and elbows protruding out to block our view of this lovely curve that sweeps down through her entire body. I'll show you what I mean. Stand over here and take the pose of the statue.

SILVIA
(Closing her blouse.)

Oh I couldn't do that.

BEN

No, I mean just the way you are.

SILVIA

You need someone bigger than me.

BEN

You're just right.

(She stands next to the statue. He instructs her in the pose, starting with her feet.)

Rest your weight on your right leg. Put your left heel down, your toes up, and bend your left leg out as far as you can. Drop your right shoulder and turn your head to the left. No, just slightly. That's it. Now reach down with your right hand as if you were holding up the gown. Your left elbow is resting on a pedestal. Your left hand is extended across in front of you, palm up. In her hand was an apple, but we'll have to imagine it.

SILVIA

An apple?

BEN

She won it in a contest.

SILVIA

I thought it was Eve who ate the apple.

BEN

She did, but the Greeks had a completely different view of the apple, For them, it was a symbol of fertility and fecundity.

SILVIA
(Falling out of the pose.)

Fe-cun-dity?

BEN

It means fruitful.

SILVIA

Fruit-ful. I see, like an apple.

BEN

Right. There's a famous Greek myth about a man who had to choose between three women, Hera – the wife of Zeus – Athena, and Aphrodite. Hera offered him power, Athena offered him wisdom, and Aphrodite offered him love.

SILVIA

Naturally he picked love.

BEN

So Paris gave Aphrodite the apple.

SILVIA

Paris. That's where I'd really like to go someday. It must be the most beautiful city in the world.

BEN

Many people think so.

SILVIA

I just love "Gigi" and watching Gene Kelly dance, you know an American in Paris. They're my favorite movies.

BEN

That was a long time ago.

SILVIA

I've got the videos, must have watched them at least a dozen times.

BEN

While you're there, you could go see the original of the Aphrodite in the Louvre. *(Pause.)* It's the big museum in Paris.

SILVIA

I'd like to just walk around the city. I've got this idea, I know it's crazy but I think I'd really feel at home, like I lived there.

BEN

The French can be very unfriendly to foreigners.

SILVIA

But I love the way they talk. Toujours l'amour. What does it mean?

BEN

Always love.

SILVIA

Toujours l'amour.

BEN

Let's get back into position. Left knee forward, drop the right shoulder, turn your head, right hand down. No, like this.

(He guides her hand down her hip.)

Bend your left elbow, arm across in front of you.

SILVIA
(*Squeezing her hand.*)

The apple goes here.

BEN

Right.

SILVIA

My nose itches.

BEN

We're almost through.

SILVIA

Can I scratch it?

BEN

No, I'll scratch it.

(*He rubs his finger along her nose.*)

SILVIA

The other side.

(*Staring into her eyes, he slides his hand across her nose and down the
other side. She drops out of the pose and grips his arm for support.*)

What does she do when her nose itches?

BEN

Gods don't get itchy noses.

SILVIA

If she's Greek, how come she's in Paris?

BEN

She was buried in an earthquake on the island of Melos soon after they installed her beside the playing field. She wasn't found until 1820, when some farmers dug her up and sold her to the French Ambassador in Constantinople. Greece was still part of Turkey in those days. After showing her off in the major ports around the eastern Mediterranean, the Ambassador brought her to France and presented her to the king, Louis XVIII, who put her in the Louvre.

SILVIA

She spent all that time buried in the ground?

BEN

About two thousand years.

SILVIA

No wonder she looks so grim.

BEN

It's ironic because Aphrodite actually came from the sea. She arose from the Mediterranean and went ashore on the island of Cyprus.

SILVIA

Just like that, she came up out of the water?

BEN

In Botticelli's famous painting, she appears just after she breaks the surface, standing on a seashell.

SILVIA

You mean he was there and saw her?

BEN

No, no, Botticelli was one of the great painters of the fifteenth century in Italy in the period just before the High Renaissance.

SILVIA

That was before Mussolini?

BEN

Mussolini?

SILVIA

Wasn't he Italian?

BEN

Yes, but he ruled Italy in this century. And his dictatorship was anything but a renaissance.

SILVIA

I'm sorry to be such a dummy. They didn't teach us any ancient history in school.

BEN

You're not unusual. Even my college students can't find Greece on the map.

SILVIA

It's somewhere near Athens. Isn't it?

BEN

Yes.

SILVIA

There's so much you could teach me.

BEN

Right now, I'd like you to get back in position.

(She quickly adopts the pose with no coaching from BEN.)

Bend your left knee forward some more.

SILVIA

I can't.

BEN

Just a little.

SILVIA

I guess I'm not built the way she is.

BEN

She has her leg out and her toes up because this pose was adopted from earlier Aphrodites who had a shield propped up on the left foot.

SILVIA

A shield? What did she need a shield for?

BEN

To protect herself, back in the days before Greece was civilized.

SILVIA

I don't think I can do this.

BEN

Let me See if I can help.

(He kneels down and tries to pull her leg forward. She loses her balance and topples over on top of him. XENIA enters, but stops when she sees the two entangled figures pause to stare into each other's eyes. SILVIA gets up and pulls BEN to his feet.)

SILVIA

Are you all right?

BEN

Fine. What about you?

SILVIA

I'm sorry, I lost my balance.

BEN

My fault entirely.

XENIA

Well, well, I see Professor that your research has broadened out somewhat, if you'll pardon the expression, and right under the statue's great big nose.

(SILVIA quickly exits. Light down on the statue.)

BEN

She came to tell me I have to exercise.

XENIA

Exercise? Aren't you supposed to do that down in the gym?

BEN

I asked her to assume the pose of Aphrodite so we could see what she would look like with arms.

XENIA

And lo suddenly you find yourself on the floor wrapped in her embrace.

BEN

She couldn't get her left knee out far enough so I tried to help her and …

XENIA

Over she went, tipped forward by those enormous Alps.

BEN

It happened so quickly …

XENIA

There you were, buried under an avalanche of Jungfrau-knockers.

BEN

I was trying to show that without her arms the statue appears as a powerful column, a figure reduced to its barest essentials, rather like a sculpture by Brancusi.

XENIA

Barest essentials, just what you were hoping to get down to.

BEN

It was all perfectly innocent.

XENIA

The look in your eye was anything but innocent.

BEN

How I conduct my research is my business and no concern of yours.

XENIA

I know you think I'm a nuisance and a pest, but I'm really very anxious for you to find what it is you're searching for.

BEN

You've made it very clear you have neither an understanding nor an appreciation of what I'm trying to do.

XENIA

I may not see the point, but it's obvious that you'll never be satisfied until you achieve your goal.

BEN

The best thing you can do is leave me alone.

XENIA

I need to warn you about Silvia.

BEN

She's a nice kid, not well educated but very eager to learn.

XENIA

She's not here to be a student.

BEN

She's asked me to teach her when I have the time.

XENIA

Knowing that professors are eager to give special lessons to students who happen to be lovely of face and figure.

BEN

That's an unwarranted insult to both of us.

XENIA

Surely this isn't the first time you've taken advantage of such a tempting situation.

(BEN starts to reply but turns away instead.)

Would it change your intentions if I told you this is not her idea?

BEN

What do you mean?

XENIA

Everything here is designed to make you into what they want you to be. You've got to be constantly on your guard and fight and fight hard to remain true to yourself.

BEN

I'm here for a purpose, and no one can stop me from accomplishing it.

XENIA

Brave words, but they're enormously clever and they usually succeed.

BEN

Like everyone else, they'll soon find that I'm stronger than they are.

XENIA

Let's hope you're right, but take this advice from a friend, trust no one.

(She exits, leaving BEN to ponder her parting words.)

Scene 6

BEN is examining the statue's outthrust left leg. Medium light on the statue. SILVIA enters.

BEN

Silvia, about yesterday, I hope you understand that I didn't mean to … it was an accident.

SILVIA

It was my fault. I lost my balance.

BEN

I shouldn't have asked you to do it, to pose like the statue.

SILVIA

That's all right. Anything I can do to help.

BEN

I don't need any right now.

SILVIA

We still don't know what she'd look like with arms.

BEN

There are a number of reconstructions, in my books.

SILVIA

I looked up the painting by that Italian painter you were telling me about.

BEN

Botticelli.

SILVIA

They call it "The Birth of Venus."

BEN

The Italians call her Venus. (Pause.) Rome was in Italy.

SILVIA

It still is…isn't it?

BEN

I mean the Roman Empire, not the city. There's that old saying you know, when in Rome.

SILVIA

When in Rome?

BEN

You do as the Romans do.

SILVIA

What's that?

BEN

Whatever.

SILVIA

Whatever?

BEN

Look, I'm very busy right now.

SILVIA

Her arms, the arms of the Venus in the painting, they really do get in the way.

BEN

Italy was still coming out of the Middle Ages, so the artists couldn't celebrate the human figure the way the ancient pagans did.

SILVIA

Pagans?

BEN

It's a term we commonly use to describe people who do not believe in god.

SILVIA

But the Greeks, they had gods.

BEN

Yes, lots of them.

SILVIA

But there's really only one.

BEN

Some people think so, some people don't.

SILVIA

If there's one, there can't be a whole lot of others too.

BEN

That raises a very profound philosophical question. And the answer is right here.

SILVIA

Here?

(Light up on the statue.)

BEN

In this figure. She's composed of a number of disparate parts and many of them, as I've pointed out, contradict each other. Yet somehow they come together to form a magnificent unity. These fragments and discordant elements fuse into a wondrous whole, so that right away we see her as a masterwork of art. The question is, which is she, the parts or the whole? Many or One? One or Many?

SILVIA

What's the answer?

BEN

I don't know. That's what I'm trying to figure out.

(He crosses to the statue.)

SILVIA

Maybe it's kind of like marriage you know when two people become one.

BEN

It's a philosophical question. It has nothing to do with marriage.

SILVIA

But she's the goddess of love …

BEN

Love is a psychological phenomenon. It's purely subjective, while what I'm searching for is a reality that exists independent of how you or I or anyone feels about it.

SILVIA

If you find this whatever it is, what do you do with it?

BEN

The goal is to discover the fundamental nature of reality, like Einstein did with his theory of relativity and astronomers have done in describing the Big Bang.

SILVIA

The Big Bang?

BEN

The point is there are certain basic truths that we can't perceive directly but that we can deduce from what we can see, and that's the challenge here. I'm convinced she has the answer, and I'm determined to find out what it is.

SILVIA

Why did you pick Aphrodite when you have no interest in what's the most important thing in anyone's life?

BEN

What's that?

SILVIA

Love.

BEN

Love?

SILVIA

How can you understand Aphrodite if you're not in love?

BEN

I'm married you know.

SILVIA

But you've come here to live by yourself.

BEN

I need to concentrate all my energies on what's turned out to be a more difficult task than I ever anticipated.

SILVIA
(Crossing to him.)

She's a woman, and it seems to me you need a woman to help find what you're looking for.

BEN

No one can help me I'm afraid.

SILVIA

She would say you are very wrong about that.

BEN

She doesn't say anything.

SILVIA

Toujours l'amour.

BEN

What?

SILVIA

Toujours l'amour, the key to unlocking the secrets she keeps hidden from those who've forgotten how to love.

(Light down on the statue.)

BEN

Look, I know what you're up to and it's not going to work. They showed you the Botticelli, and they told you to come in here and question why I chose Aphrodite so you could talk about love and all this nonsense about toujours l'amour.

SILVIA

No.

BEN

They're using you to distract me from my research. Why?

SILVIA

I don't know what you're talking about.

BEN

You can tell them I know what they're trying to do and you can stop pretending to be this innocent young girl who's curious to know about things your devious little mind could never begin to comprehend.

SILVIA

I don't know where you got these crazy ideas but they're totally false. I do want to learn and I do want to help you.

BEN

I don't need your help.

SILVIA

Please, tell me what this is all about.

BEN

You know perfectly well.

SILVIA

All I know is.. .1 love you.

BEN

It's no good Silvia.

SILVIA

What do I have to do to prove it?

BEN

Tell me the truth.

SILVIA

The truth is somebody's been telling you a whole bunch of lies.

BEN

Apparently so.

(He turns to the statue. She clutches his arm.)

SILVIA

It's not me.

(He shoves her away with such force that she falls back onto the couch.)

You're more than just a brain you know. You've got feelings just like everybody else, I know I've seen it in your eyes, in the way they're searching for something, trying to find what's been lost inside.

(She rises.)

Don't you see? I can give you what you need to become the fine and wonderful person you really are.

BEN

Very fancy language all of a sudden. Did they write it for you?

SILVIA

They're my words and if they sound unusual it's because they come from right here *(her heart)*.

BEN

I don't want to hear anymore.

SILVIA

Don't you understand? I love you.

(He advances toward her.)

You've got to believe me.

BEN

Get out.

SILVIA

Before it's too late.

(She exits, leaving him staring after her.)

SCENE 7

BEN is sitting on the couch reading a book. Medium light on the statue. SILVIA enters carrying a tray with a pitcher of martinis and two glasses. She places the tray on the table and fills both glasses.

BEN

Two glasses?

SILVIA

This one's for your wife.

BEN

My wife?

SILVIA

She called to say she'd be here at five.

BEN
(Rising.)

She's coming here, now?

SILVIA

Should be here any minute.

BEN

Good lord.

SILVIA

You don't want to see her?

BEN

Yes, yes, of course.

SILVIA

Shall I tell her to wait?

BEN

No, no, it's just that I you know wasn't expecting her.

(SILVIA leaves. BEN picks up his jacket and puts it on. HELEN enters.)

HELEN

Hello Ben, I thought this would be a good time to celebrate.

BEN

Celebrate? Celebrate what?

HELEN

Here's a toast, to my new job.

BEN

Congratulations, what is it?

HELEN

I'm going to write a story for television.

BEN

Television?

HELEN

It's for a series on what women have had to do to survive in a man's world.

BEN

Isn't that kind of old hat by now?

HELEN

This will be a completely new approach. We'll go back and find women who faced very difficult situations and came up with ingenious ways to overcome them.

BEN

More women as scheming Lucretia Borgias? Isn't one Hillary Clinton enough?

HELEN

These will be stories about ordinary women doing extraordinary things.

BEN

Ordinary women? Who cares about ordinary women?

HELEN

Ordinary women. A lot of them still need role models so they'll know how to cope with their own difficulties.

BEN

Look, I'm glad you came. There's something we need to discuss.

HELEN

Let me tell you what I found, in the attic, a box full of papers about my great grandmother. It's quite a story. Grandmamere first married a doctor who turned out to be an abusive alcoholic. He died suddenly, under mysterious circumstances. His family was convinced she had killed him.

BEN

Grandmamere murdered her husband?

HELEN

We don't know for sure, but now left with two young sons and no money, she proceeded to marry the richest man in the county who soon died.

BEN

She killed him too?

HELEN

He was an elderly judge who apparently passed away of natural causes. When they found his will, instead of his estate going to his heirs by his first wife, there was a codicil giving everything to grandmamere. The only trouble was the codicil had been forged, by grandmamere.

BEN

A murderer and a forger?

HELEN

She was guilty and everyone knew it, but the Governor of the state came along, pardoned her, and married her. So she married the first time for love, the second time for money, and the third time to stay out of prison.

BEN

No one's going to believe any of this.

HELEN

I know how implausible it sounds, but I have proof that it's all true – the court records, newspaper clippings, letters, diaries, all from that box in the attic.

BEN

I knew marrying into your family was risky, but I didn't know it contained killer genes in the female line.

HELEN

She did it all for the sake of her sons.

BEN

I would think you'd want this ghost to stay firmly locked up in that box in the attic.

HELEN

George thinks it's a wonderful story.

BEN

George.

HELEN

He says he'll get a friend of his who's a cable TV producer to put it into the series on women I was just telling you about.

BEN

What's George know about the television business?

HELEN

It's amazing the number of people he knows in the entertainment world.

BEN

Is that why he's always in New York instead of at the University where they're paying him to be a full-time Dean?

HELEN

He's doing a great job in promoting the school and in raising money from all the contacts he's developed in the city.

BEN

If he loves New York so much, why doesn't he live there?

HELEN

His wife doesn't like New York, hates it in fact.

BEN

Since they're separated, let him go live there and then I can come home. The situation here has become impossible with all the interruptions and distractions.

HELEN

Why can't you just ignore them like you ignore everything else when you're at home?

BEN

I can't stay here any longer.

HELEN

It takes a while to get adjusted to anyplace that's new.

BEN

You've got to get George to move out, go somewhere else.

HELEN

We're going to work together on the story about grandmamere. Being an English professor, he can help me give it real dramatic flow.

BEN

It's dramatic enough without any help from him.

HELEN

You're the world's leading expert on Aphrodite BEN and now you're on the verge of discovering things that no one else has ever imagined. The book will be celebrated everywhere ideas are taken seriously.

(BEN turns to the statue.)

And now that you're in the ideal place to do your research, you complain that the conditions here aren't exactly what you want them to be. You've forgotten how difficult it was when you were trying to work at home and at school. Keep concentrating on what's important and you'll soon find everything you've been searching for.

BEN

(Filling his glass. Light up on the statue.)

I just discovered something yesterday that no one's ever noticed before. In order for the left leg to come out this far, it has to be longer than her right leg. To produce this beautiful movement of the robe across here, the sculptor had to make one leg longer than the other one.

(He circles the statue.)

Another example of a flawed part that somehow joins with others to form a magnificent whole.

(HELEN quietly leaves.)

Isn't that man's greatest achievement, to create order out of chaos, meaning out of meaninglessness?

(XENIA enters. Absorbed in the statue, BEN ignores her.)

XENIA

Got to be something wrong when someone walks away from a very dry martini.

(She holds up HELEN'S half-filled glass.)

I wonder sometimes what would happen if all the alcohol in the world suddenly turned into gold. Instead of drinking it, you get to spend it, on anything your heart desires. Me, I'd buy a boat, load it up with my favorite people and off we'd go, Cannes, Nice, Capri, Corfu, day after day of sun, sea, and sex.

(She drinks.)

But then something happens. You begin to notice that something's missing. You feel inside you a terrible emptiness that keeps pressing against your chest and your head until you can't stand it anymore and someone hands you a glass filled not with gold but with a cold dry liquid fire that burns away that terrible thing inside and the pain goes away. So here's to the divine elixir that is infinitely more precious than gold.

(She drinks. BEN remains totally absorbed in the statue.)

Don't you ever feel that inside there's this great big black hole? No you wouldn't. You've always got her. The Great Sphinx who knows all and says nothing. What would happen if we loaded her up with some gin – no, she's a wine type, Greek, that's all they had back then, good god can you imagine. Fill her up till the wine softens her brain and loosens her tongue and listen. Listen very carefully.

                         BEN
What?

                         XENIA
She's trying to speak.

                         BEN
I don't hear anything.

                         XENIA
Shhhh.

   (*She crosses to the statue and lifts her head toward Aphrodite's face.*)

It's hard to make out with her accent. (*Pause.*) She wants to know if you love her.

                         BEN
What?

                         XENIA
Do you love her?

   (*BEN gazes at the statue. Both stand in frozen silence as the light fades.*)

SCENE 8

The room is dark.

BEN

What? Who is it? Who's there?

(Lights up. BEN, in his pajamas, appears at left.)

You? The middle of the night and now you're lonesome for some company. But of course, that's what nights are for aren't they? Toujours l'amour. Love über alles. Well you're wasting your time with me. I've given you everything I have, everything, and what do I get in return? Nothing, zero, zilch, nada, nothing. You who we've worshiped for two thousand years as the goddess of love, you're a fraud, a cruel trick of the gods to fool us into believing you have some wondrous power far beyond anything possessed by us mere mortals. But it's a lie. You're a cold, selfish, stony-hearted woman who gives nothing of yourself to anyone, and I'm going to expose you for what you really are. No longer will anyone swoon under your diabolical spell. No longer will anyone give themselves up to your strangling embrace. Do you hear me? Do you understand?

(He circles the statue.)

What? What did you say? You want your arms? Does your nose itch? *(He laughs.)* You don't have to drive or use the telephone, do you? Think how tired they'll get, especially this one sticking out there in front of you.

(He angles his left arm across in front of her. He opens his palm and there appears an apple in his hand.)

What's this? An Apple? For me? You're giving me an apple? Why? An apple a day keeps the doctor away, but at night? What good's an apple in the middle of the night?

(SILVIA appears in a negligee and quickly assumes the pose of the statue. She extends her left hand and beckons to BEN. He crosses to her. She caresses his neck and chest and takes the apple.)

XENIA
(From the shadows.)

Professor.

(SILVIA and BEN freeze. XENIA crosses and takes the apple from SILVIA.)

Don't you know never to trust a woman with an apple?

(SILVIA retreats into the shadows.)

I warned you about her.

(BEN reaches for the apple but XENIA clutches it to her chest and crosses behind the couch.)

HELEN
(From the shadows.)

Ben.

(XENIA and BEN freeze. HELEN takes the apple from XENIA.)

Who is this woman?

(XENIA retreats into the shadows.)

BEN

I don't know.

HELEN

You don't know?

BEN

She drops by occasionally.

HELEN

You're supposed to be concentrating on the statue.

BEN

I've learned all I need to know.

HELEN

No, there's more, much more.

BEN

I've got to get out of here.

HELEN

You must persist and not let anything stop you.

BEN

I'm finished.

HELEN

I know you can do it.

XENIA

But he can't do it alone.

(She takes the apple.)

SILVIA

Don't listen to that crazy old witch.

(She grabs the apple.)

I am the one who loves you.

XENIA
(Grabbing the apple.)

Love will blind him to the truth.

HELEN
(Taking the apple.)

Six months darling, that's all, six months.

(Music, soft at first. The three women dance around BEN, passing the apple from one to the other. Their dancing becomes ever more rapid and frenzied in tempo with the quickening rhythms of the music. Lights out. A scream pierces the darkness, followed by another. Lights up. BEN is lying on the couch twisting and turning as he calls out once again. SILVIA rushes to his side.)

SILVIA

What's the matter? Are you all right?

BEN

Silvia.

SILVIA
(Feeling his brow.)

You're hot. I'll go get some aspirin.

BEN
(Grabbing her hand.)

No, no, don't leave me.

SILVIA

You've got a fever.

BEN

There were these women dancing around.

SILVIA

Just lie down and take it easy.

BEN

All fighting for the apple.

SILVIA

The apple?

BEN

Aphrodite's apple.

SILVIA

You had Aphrodite's apple?

BEN

You took it, and then Xenia and Helen.

SILVIA

Xenia and Helen?

BEN

All three of you, fighting for the apple, dancing round and round. I'd never seen you like that, wild and wanton …

SILVIA

Yes.

BEN

Like a woman afire …

SILVIA

Yes, yes.

BEN

With passion and desire.

SILVIA

Yes, yes, yes.

(She crawls on top of him. Music. Lights down on the couch, up on Aphrodite.)

SCENE 9

BEN, wearing grey slacks and a button-down shirt, is sitting on the couch, his face buried in his hands. Medium light on the statue. XENIA enters.

XENIA

Good morning. Oh, not so good. Bad night? I know how it is. Sometimes in the morning you ache all over, trying to forget the demons of the night. The demons that haunt the night. Some are old and ugly and make terrifying noises, but some are young and beautiful and sing a sweet siren's song. A song no man can resist, certainly not one who is seeking to know the innermost secrets of Aphrodite.

BEN
(Head still bowed.)

I'm in no mood to talk.

XENIA

I'm afraid you've got some explaining to do. We know she was here.

BEN

No.

XENIA

She's not supposed to make visits when she's off duty.

BEN
(Raising his head.)

I was having this nightmare. She came to see if I was all right.

XENIA

I have nightmares but no one comes in to comfort me.

BEN

I must have called out in my dream.

XENIA

A dream come true when she comes bringing her mountains to Mohammed, an offering you were unable to resist.

BEN

No.

XENIA

I don't want to hear the sordid details. You can wait and explain them to the Director.

BEN

The Director?

XENIA

The Director will need to know the facts in order to determine the appropriate punishment. Sleeping with the guests is strictly prohibited.

BEN

She didn't sleep …

XENIA

Nor did you from what I can see.

BEN

You don't understand.

XENIA

The rules are very clear. She'll have to be dismissed.

BEN

Dismissed? No.

XENIA

Since no one knows about this yet, the Director would prefer that it not become the subject of a public investigation and is willing to overlook it this time if assured it won't happen again.

BEN

Don't worry.

XENIA

But someone must be here with you to guarantee there are no more such incidents.

BEN

Someone? Here?

XENIA

You've got three rooms. There's plenty of space. And I won't interfere with your work.

BEN.
(Rising.)

You're planning to move in here? No, it's impossible, totally out of the question.

XENIA

Then the Director will have no choice but to fire her.

BEN

She didn't…it wasn't her fault.

XENIA

All the more reason someone needs to keep an eye on you.

BEN

You can't, goddammit no.

XENIA

You'll find that I can be a great help in your research.

BEN

I don't need your help, I don't need anything from you.

XENIA

Let me remind you about something you seem to have forgotten. She can be very dangerous to your health.

BEN

Silvia?

XENIA

Aphrodite.

BEN

Aphrodite?

(Light up on the statue.)

XENIA

Let's suppose she doesn't think you're worthy of learning her innermost secrets. What does she do? She can't run away or slap your face or tell you to go to hell. Yet you persist in wanting to know her, to possess her, to invade and violate her very being. Her only recourse is to use her extraordinary power to tempt you with someone she knows you'll be unable to resist.

BEN

I thought you said it was the Director who was behind this plot to divert me from my research.

XENIA

She's merely trying to protect Aphrodite.

BEN

She? The Director is a woman?

XENIA

Haven't you noticed, there are no men here.

BEN

No men. Only women?

XENIA

You're very fortunate they let you in.

BEN

It's become more impossible every day. I've got to get out of here.

XENIA

You'd go off and leave her?

BEN

I've learned all I'm going to learn.

XENIA

You can't quit now when you're so close to achieving your goal.

BEN

She'll only reveal what she wants to reveal.

XENIA

But there's something about her that's so obvious I'm surprised you've overlooked it.

BEN

Believe me, I've considered every conceivable possibility.

XENIA

Isn't it true that she was created by a man?

BEN

Yes.

XENIA

So what she represents is not a woman but your own grandiose and distorted vision of what a woman should be. There's really no mystery here. When you look at her, you're actually looking at yourself, and if you look carefully enough you'll discover the grotesque and misshapen thing we might call the essence of man.

BEN

The essence of man? That's the most ridiculous statement I've ever heard.

XENIA

You see her as an ideal, but it's something you've invented so you can feel superior to us by claiming that men can conceive of these dazzling mirages and women can't. She tells us a great deal about the absurdity of the male mind but nothing at all about women.

BEN

It's not women I'm interested in. It's the truth.

XENIA

I'm telling you the truth, which if you're half as intelligent as I think you are, you'll soon begin to understand.

BEN
(Turning to the statue.)

The essence of man?

XENIA

Think about it while I go and bring over my things.

(She leaves. BEN slowly circles the statue, sinks onto the couch, and buries his head in his hands.)

Scene 10

Scattered about the room are boxes on which are piled dresses, skirts, sweaters, and coats, topped by an assortment of hats. A quilt and a pillow are strewn across the couch. BEN folds up the quilt and slams the pillow down on top of it. Medium light on the statue. SILVIA enters carrying a brightly colored scarf.

SILVIA

This must be hers. I found it in back of her closet.

BEN

Don't bring it in here. There's no room for even a string bikini.

SILVIA
(Laughing.)

I can't see Xenia in a string bikini.

BEN

God knows she's got everything else.

SILVIA
(Crossing among the boxes.)

What a collection of stuff.

(She holds up an elegant evening cape.)

Where would you wear something like this?

BEN

La Scala perhaps.

SILVIA

La Scala?

BEN

It's the opera house in Milan.

SILVIA

She's got something for just about anything anywhere.

BEN

And more shoes than Imelda Marcos ever imagined.

SILVIA
(Trying on a hat.)

This looks like something my grandmother would wear.

BEN

Better not let Xenia hear you say that.

SILVIA

All these clothes and all she wears is that ugly black dress.

BEN

I don't know, it gives her a touch of elegance.

SILVIA

Elegance?

BEN

In an understated kind of way.

SILVIA

You like her?

BEN

No.

SILVIA

Then why did you let her move in with you?

BEN

Look, you keep the scarf. She'll never miss it.

SILVIA

I thought the other night, what you said, I thought you meant it.

BEN

I did.

SILVIA

Then how can you live here with her?

BEN

She's going to help with my research.

SILVIA

Help? How can she help?

BEN

She's full of interesting ideas.

SILVIA

I know she's very intelligent, but most of the time what she says doesn't make any sense.

BEN

Occasionally it does.

SILVIA

But you don't have to live with her.

BEN

Don't worry, she sleeps on the couch.

SILVIA

I can't go on like this, only seeing you when she's not here.

BEN

We'll give her some bad gin and send her to the infirmary.

SILVIA

I'm serious.

BEN

She'll soon realize she's made a mistake and want her own place back.

SILVIA

No, there's something going on and I want to know what it is.

BEN

There's nothing going on.

SILVIA

Okay, you want her, that's the end of us.

BEN

I'm telling you, she's here to help with my research.

SILVIA

You're lying.

BEN

It's true.

SILVIA

I don't believe it.

(She crosses upstage.)

BEN

Where are you going?

SILVIA

Out of here and out of your life.

BEN

Wait a minute. Here's what happened. She found out about the other night when I was having my nightmare. She said they'd fire you unless she could move in here to see that nothing like that happened again.

SILVIA

You did it so I wouldn't lose my job?

BEN

I couldn't bear to see you leave.

SILVIA

Then you do love me?

(She throws the scarf around his shoulders, pulls him to her, and gives him a passionate kiss. He responds with increasing enthusiasm.)

I've got a plan to get us both out of here. We'll go away where no one can find us, where you'll be able to write your book with no one to bother you.

BEN

But I haven't finished my research.

SILVIA

You won't need her. I'll he your Aphrodite.

(Noises offstage.)

Tomorrow we go, tomorrow.

(She gives him a quick kiss and dashes off. BEN takes the scarf, caresses it tenderly, drapes it over the shoulders of the statue, and steps back to admire his handiwork. XENIA enters carrying a bottle and two glasses.)

XENIA

I brought us some champagne to celebrate.

BEN

Celebrate?

XENIA

Four days together, four wonderful days.

BEN

For you.

XENIA

Come on, you've got more done in these four days than you have in weeks.

BEN

I came up with some new ideas.

XENIA

And where did you get those ideas?

(She fills the glasses.)

Here's to day four and many many more.

(She drinks, he doesn't.)

Oh I'm sorry. I left the couch a mess, but I wanted to get out of your way so you could get to work early this morning.

BEN

You left your towel soaking wet on the bathroom floor.

XENIA

I was in a hurry.

BEN

And your hairpins were all over the sink.

XENIA

It won't happen again, I promise.

BEN

And all these clothes, it's like living in a warehouse.

XENIA

I can't bear to throw anything away. Each one brings back a very special memory.

(She puts on a straw hat.)

Tangiers, when it was full of really creative people, not the phonies who go there now.

(She holds up a sweater.)

St. Moritz, when it had real class and wasn't overrun by bankers and businessmen. And this scarf, that glorious September in Capri.

BEN

Capri?

XENIA

It was unseasonably cold and someone gave me this scarf.

BEN

Someone?

XENIA

I always liked to make friends with the natives. Made it feel more like home.

BEN

So there was always someone?

XENIA

In Morocco once I tried living alone but I didn't know how to say "no" in Arabic.

BEN

I'm sure they would have understood "no" in French.

XENIA

French? One never says "no" in French.

(She fills her glass and crosses to him. She drinks, he sips.)

BEN

Well I'm saying "no" in English, no to your moving in here where you're neither welcome nor wanted.

XENIA

You look at a seed and wonder what can come of this ugly little thing and then watch it grow into a gorgeous flower. So here's to us and the beginning of a beautiful friendship.

BEN

A seed needs water to nurture its growth, not bottles of booze.

XENIA

There's the old saying you know, two heads are better than one.

BEN

And there's the law of physics that says no two bodies can occupy the same space at the same time.

XENIA

Even when they want to?

BEN

Never.

XENIA

What does science know about two people who need each other?

BEN

I'm just stating a simple fact.

XENIA

Facts are merely the bars that imprison ordinary minds. For us, there are no such limits. We are free to soar wherever our imaginations take us.

(Light up on the statue.)

You claim she contains the answers to questions no one has yet been able to discover. She is the invisible made visible, an object that appears before us like some visitor from a universe more real than the shadow world we see all around us. You may be right, but how can you prove it? What scientific test can you apply that will demonstrate that what you claim is true?

BEN

In my book, I'll make it clear in my book.

XENIA

Clear to you but perhaps to no one else.

BEN

It won't be easy, I'm very much aware of that.

XENIA

Convince me and then you'll know it's true.

BEN

You?

XENIA
(Tapping his glass with hers.)

There's no hurry, We've got lots of time.

(She drinks. He pauses and then slowly takes a sip.)

Scene 11

XENIA is rummaging through some of the boxes. She pulls out a flaming red dress and clasps it tightly as she stomps the floor in a flamenco dance. Medium light on the statue. HELEN appears. Still dancing, XENIA turns upstage. Seeing HELEN, she slams her feet down even more vigorously.

HELEN

Excuse me. Where is Professor Hastings? Please, I need to see my husband. This is his room isn't it?

XENIA
(Still dancing.)

Seville, city of flaming fires burning through the night.

HELEN

My husband.

XENIA

But all fires turn to ash.

HELEN

Where is he?

XENIA
(Stopping her dance.)

One glorious night and I never saw him again.

HELEN

What are all these boxes doing here?

XENIA
(Crossing among the boxes.)

Manuel, Seville. Giacomo, Taormina, Ahmad, Cairo. Surachai, Bangkok.

HELEN

These are all yours?

XENIA

Wu Ching, Singapore. They're all Chinese in Singapore you know. They've got no hair. It'.s like making love to a young boy. He gave me this. *(She puts on a Chinese coolie hat.)*

HELEN

You're living here?

XENIA
(Affecting a Chinese accent.)

Only way to keep man is marry him.

HELEN

Would you mind telling me just what is going on here?

XENIA

But maybe not so.

HELEN

Where is Professor Hastings?

XENIA

Why you bring him here?

HELEN

He needed a place to do his research.

XENIA

This place no good, full of funny people.

HELEN

The doctor said this was the best place for treating his kind of condition.

XENIA

Ah.

HELEN

They thought it could be done in six months.

XENIA
(Laughing.)

Yah.

HELEN

But he's improved faster than anyone expected, so I've come to take him home.

XENIA

He like it here.

HELEN

He's been wanting to come home for some time.

XENIA

Time change.

HELEN

Look, just tell me where I can find him.

XENIA

Not here now.

HELEN

Is he all right?

XENIA

Sometime.

HELEN

Sometimes?

XENIA

Some days okay.

HELEN

He'll be fine when I get him home.

XENIA

You love him?

HELEN

Love him? Of course I love him.

XENIA

Too bad.

HELEN

Why do you say that?

(XENIA drops the hat on the couch and leaves. HELEN crosses among the boxes, examining the piles of clothes and hats. BEN enters.)

BEN

Helen. What are you doing here?

HELEN

Admiring the wardrobe of your new roommate.

BEN

You should have told me you were coming.

HELEN

I met her.

BEN

Xenia?

HELEN

I walked in and here she was holding this dress and pretending to be a flamenco dancer.

BEN

Her glorious night in Seville.

HELEN

Then she put on this hat and pretended to be Chinese.

BEN

Her Singapore fling.

HELEN

She's a total loony.

BEN

A bit eccentric, yes.

HELEN

How long has she been here?

BEN

It's only a temporary arrangement, until they can find another place for her.

HELEN

I can't believe you'd let someone move in here with you.

BEN

They were desperate for space.

HELEN

And a woman, a woman.

BEN

Don't worry, she sleeps on the couch.

HELEN

And you think that makes it all right?

BEN

I'm just trying to help them out in a crunch.

HELEN

Well you won't have to put up with this any longer. I'm here to take you home.

BEN

Home?

HELEN

George is gone. All that talk of his getting me a producer for my story about grandmamere, it was a lie. He kept encouraging me, leading me on thinking …well no matter, he's gone.

BEN

George.

HELEN

He's worse than you or anyone else ever thought.

BEN

You and George.

HELEN

I've thrown him out.

BEN

Right there, in my own house.

HELEN

No.

BEN

You planned it all, you and George.

HELEN

You were sick Ben and needed help. You were so obsessed with the statue that you withdrew into yourself and paid no attention to me. It was like living with a stranger and I couldn't go on like that. I talked to several doctors and finally one of them said I should send you here where they specialize in really unusual cases. And it's worked darling, you're so much better.

BEN

Six months. You and George.

HELEN

I didn't know anything about his separation before you came here. My only goal was to get you well.

BEN

And now you want me to come home as if nothing had happened.

HELEN

I love you Ben, I always have and I always will. It's been difficult, difficult for both of us, but we've learned a lot and now we can appreciate each other even more than we did before.

BEN

There's still so much to do.

HELEN

We can set it up at home any way you like so you can work without anyone bothering you.

BEN

She'll have to be in the living room.

HELEN

We'll take out the couch to give you more space.

BEN

And you'll be there to cook?

HELEN

Of course.

BEN

I haven't had a decent meal since I got here.

HELEN

I'll fix all your favorites, chicken florentine, spaghetti carbonara.

BEN

Beef bourgignon.

HELEN

With plenty of noodles.

BEN

Your special lasagna.

HELEN

And then for dessert.

BEN

Strawberry shortcake.

HELEN
(Crossing to him.)

I had something even better in mind.

(She embraces him and gives him a passionate kiss.)

BEN

You've changed your hair.

HELEN

Tomorrow, it'll be back the way you like it.

BEN

Why don't you leave it the way it is.

HELEN

Are you sure?

BEN

You never looked lovelier.

HELEN

It's so good to hold you again.

BEN

I think I've lost at least ten pounds.

HELEN

I'll go see the Director and make the arrangements. You be ready to leave when I get back.

(She exits. BEN crosses around the room, picks up XENIA'S red dress and Chinese hat and tosses them back onto the boxes. SILVIA enters.)

SILVIA

It's all set. My friend is on guard this afternoon. She says be ready to go in half an hour.

BEN

What?

SILVIA

You pretend to be sick. I'll come to take you to the infirmary and then we'll slip out a back door where my car will be waiting. We'll drive up to a friend's place in the Catskills just for the night while we decide where we want to go.

BEN

Silvia, let's slow down here a minute.

SILVIA

I couldn't sleep all last night just thinking about it.

BEN

I have to tell you something.

SILVIA
(Crossing to him.)

Just you and me together in a house all by ourselves.

BEN

I just had a visit from my wife.

SILVIA

Don't worry, we'll find a place where she'll never find us.

BEN

The situation has changed.

SILVIA

Out in the country with no one else around.

BEN

The Dean has left.

SILVIA

Not too far out of course. You'll need a library and some bookstores.

BEN

I warned her about him but she wouldn't listen.

SILVIA

But you don't really need them anymore you know. You can get everything you want on the Internet.

BEN

The Internet?

SILVIA

You get a computer and you can tap into anyplace in the world.

(She slides her arms up to his shoulders.)

I'll get a job and you'll have all day to work with no one to bother you. In the evening you can teach me everything you know. That's a lot better than going to college. And then at night there's the best part of all.

(She kisses him hungrily. He steps back and tumbles over the back of the couch. She grabs on and they both roll off the couch onto the floor. After kissing his mouth, cheek, and chin, she rises to her feet.)

I'll go down and check that the coast is clear. Remember, you have to pretend you're sick.

(She leaves. BEN tries to climb onto the couch but falls back moaning in pain. XENIA enters.)

XENIA

What's the matter? What are you doing on the floor? *(She helps him up onto the couch.)*

BEN

Easy, easy.

XENIA

Where does it hurt?

(BEN taps his chest and lies down on the couch.)

I'll go call the doctor.

BEN

No, no, I'll be all right.

XENIA

Did you fall down?

BEN

Just let me lie here a minute.

(She lifts his arm to feel his pulse.)

Owww

XENIA

There's a pain in your arm? Could be a heart attack. Don't move and I'll go get the doctor.

(She leaves. BEN sits up but immediately plunges his head down between his legs. HELEN enters.)

HELEN

Ben, what's the matter?

BEN

Dizzy.

HELEN

What?

BEN

Feeling a little dizzy.

HELEN

Dizzy?

BEN

Tried to get up too fast.

HELEN

Are you ready?

BEN

Ready?

HELEN

You're supposed to be packed up and ready to go.

BEN

Go?

HELEN

We're going home.

BEN

Home?

HELEN

I'm taking you home.

(He collapses back onto the couch. She feels his forehead.)

You're hot. You're sweating.

BEN

I'm all right.

HELEN

Come on, I'll drive you home, put you to bed, and call Dr. Schmidt.

(She tries to pull him up but he cries out and clutches his chest.)

A pain in your chest. I told you to take your blood-pressure pills.

(SILVIA enters.)

He's having a heart attack.

SILVIA

I'll take him to the infirmary.

(XENIA enters.)

XENIA

He should stay right where he is.

HELEN

We need a doctor.

SILVIA

There's a doctor in the infirmary.

XENIA

You don't move a man who's having a heart attack.

HELEN

He could die if we leave him here.

SILVIA

The infirmary's just downstairs.

(SILVIA and HELEN pull BEN to his feet. Supported by the two women, BEN walks slowly upstage. XENIA turns off the lamp and follows them out. Light up on the statue.)

Scene 12

BEN, looking drawn and pale in a bathrobe and slippers, is sitting on the couch. The room is bare, the way it was before XENIA moved in. Medium light on the statue. SILVIA enters carrying a pitcher of martinis and a glass on a tray. She sets the tray on the table and fills the glass.

SILVIA

The doctor says you can start drinking again, but only one glass.

(BEN takes the glass and slowly raises it to his lips. SILVIA lifts an envelope from the tray.)

You got a letter from your wife.

BEN

My wife?

(Lights up on HELEN.)

HELEN

Ben darling, I'm glad to hear you're feeling better. The doctor says there's no permanent damage to the heart. Just take it easy for a while and you'll be back good as new. Sorry I haven't been to see you this week, but things are happening so fast I don't seem to have time for anything. I've rented a little apartment just off Sheridan Square down in the Village. It turns out George does know a TV producer who wants to buy the story about grandmamere if we actually show her poisoning her first husband. George thinks it's a good idea because it will heighten the drama right at the beginning ...

(BEN suddenly coughs and gasps for breath. Lights down on HELEN.)

SILVIA

Are you all right?

(BEN hands her the half-filled glass.)

Maybe you can finish it later. Have they told you? I'm leaving.

BEN

Leaving?

SILVIA

To go to college.

BEN

College?

SILVIA

You always said I should.

BEN

You're leaving?

SILVIA

You made me realize how important it is to get an education.

(She takes his hand.)

I'll never be able to thank you enough for all you've done for me.

BEN

You can't leave.

SILVIA

I'll come to see you. Christmas.

BEN

Christmas?

SILVIA

Promise. Thanks again. For everything.

(She kisses him lightly on the cheek and leaves.)

BEN

Christmas?

(He sinks down into his robe. XENIA enters.)

XENIA

Well, what's the great thought for today?

BEN

She's leaving.

XENIA

Ah yes, the Alps are headed north. I'm sure they'll love them in Heidelberg.

BEN

Heidelberg?

XENIA

Isn't that the German university town?

BEN

She's going to Heidelberg?

XENIA

I lived in Germany once. Munich. There was this Bavarian count, had a castle out in the country but was too poor to keep it up, so he made his living as an artist, painting women in all kinds of sexy costumes. He liked me because he had to use all his ingenuity to transform me into a tramp.

BEN

She shouldn't go to Germany.

XENIA

Trouble was of course he made me so alluring he couldn't finish the painting. Makes you wonder how Rubens and Renoir ever managed to complete theirs.

BEN

Berenson once said, the east begins at the Rhine.

(She exits downstage left.)

You know Berenson? They called him B.B. Great connoisseur of Renaissance art, Italian Renaissance art. Had a terrific eye. Wrote some wonderful books. Sold his services to the dealers, prostituted himself to live the grand life surrounded by magnificent works of art. I've often wondered ...

(XENIA returns wearing a white fur coat.)

Was it worth the price?

XENIA

The price? I have no idea. He gave it to me.

BEN

What?

XENIA

The count, the count I was telling you about. He especially liked me in white fur.

(She twirls around and crosses to him.)

He wanted to marry me, but of course he couldn't, not a woman of the night.

BEN

A woman of the night?

XENIA

That's what he called me.

BEN

You look very nice.

XENIA

I would have made a fantastic countess, don't you think?

BEN

Yes.

XENIA

The belle of Bavaria.

BEN

Bavaria?

XENIA

It's beautiful there, especially in the winter.

(She crosses upstage.)

BEN

Where are you going?

XENIA

For a walk, in the snow.

BEN

It's winter already?

XENIA

It's time for you to go to work.

BEN

Work?

XENIA

Have you found what you were searching for?

(BEN gazes at the statue.)

The women have all left. There's no one to distract you now

(She kisses him lightly on the cheek and walks upstage.)

BEN
(Rising.)

Wait, don't go …

XENIA

You don't need me anymore.

BEN

They're gone. There's no one here.

XENIA

Just you and Aphrodite.

(Light up on the statue.)

BEN

Aphrodite.

(XENIA exits. BEN turns to the statue.)

So you've sent them all away. There's no one to protect you now.

(He sits, raises his glass.)

Just you and me. No more of your tricks. I want the truth.

(He sits staring at the statue.)

END OF PLAY